Want Your Child to Read?

A roadmap to help your
child read 1 ½ to 2 years
ABOVE grade level

LAURIE BERLANT

BA, MS Elementary Education

Want Your Child to Read?

A roadmap to help your child read 1 ½ to 2 years ABOVE grade level

Contents

Want Your Child to Read?

What parent doesn't? The challenge comes in knowing where to start and what road to follow.

There is a lot of material available that makes claims of being able to teach your child to read. Which one do you choose? This book is designed to help you make an informed decision and to offer an exact road map for your child's success.

The good news is that every road to success in any business or venture follows a specific pattern and design. Brilliant and extremely successful people will tell you that if you follow the design and take the steps, you will succeed.

Reading is no different. I will give you the map. I will make available to you everything you need to help you teach your child to read. All you need to do is follow the design, take the steps and your child will read!

Are you ready to give your child the most important gift? ...... *the ability to read.*

Why You Should Read this Book

This book has been written especially for parents. It addresses many of the questions that I have been asked over the years. It looks at several different ways of teaching reading and will hopefully give parents insight into the choices they have on how to teach their child to read.

In a nutshell, learning to read is a science. Not an exact science (like math), for English is a language that has many 'exceptions' to the rule, but there is an exact pattern or let's say 'roadmap' to follow for success.

By following this roadmap, most of my students ended the school year reading one and a half to two years ABOVE grade level! Isn't that great? Wouldn't you like that to be your child?

This book offers a guide to how and when to teach your child to read, develop a love of reading and ultimately help them be successful in school.

And isn't that what you want for them?

Let me Introduce Myself

Hi, my name is Laurie Berlant. I have both my bachelor's and master's degrees in Elementary Education. I taught elementary school for many years, and I am a reading specialist.

A little background….

I started teaching right after graduating college. I taught fifth grade. When I looked at my students' reading tests, patterns seemed to be emerging. There were those who did well. Those who could read the words but struggled with comprehension and those who struggled just to read the words.

My answer to the best way to teach my class was to divide them into ability groups so they could all reach their potential. This was the start of my choice to become a reading specialist.

The next year I taught third grade. I found the same patterns. The following year, I requested a position in first grade. I wanted the opportunity to start the kids off on the right track.

My years in first grade were wonderful. As much as I taught the kids, they challenged me. I learned that 'traditional methods' have pre-requisites that MUST be in place before you can even begin to teach how to read. I learned that the road you put your children's feet on must be crystal clear.

And more importantly, it must be consistent and prepare them for any 'exceptions' that come.

I was also a director at several tutoring centers. It was my job to evaluate children who came in for reading help. In every case, I was looking at the same deficiencies, the same patterns.

I spent most of my teaching career in first grade. I designed materials and wrote curriculum. I developed a reading system that works. It develops skills, increases the ability to work independently and builds confidence. And when kids come across an 'exception', they know exactly what to do.

With its implementation, my students succeeded. In fact, as I mentioned earlier, most of my students ended the year reading one and half to two years ABOVE grade level!

How do you think the kids felt when they realized what they could do?

How proud of their kids do you think their parents were?

How would you feel if that was your child?

Reading Strategies

Long ago, in a galaxy far away, as my children will say, parents did not teach their children to read, that was what school was for. Most children went into first grade not knowing how to read.

Things have changed!

Parents are more involved with their children and as more children are attending pre-school, day care and VPK, children are being introduced earlier to the beginning fundamentals of learning to read. All for the best!

Then there is the 'internet'. A world of knowledge became unlocked with our access to it. However, as I searched for 'teach your child to read', I was amazed by what I found.

I found: Your child can read in one week, your one-year-old can be reading, learning to read is a 'natural process' that will happen by itself etc.

I found the continual use and simplification of reading terms – ex: sight words, cvc, whole language, word families disconcerting. I read about not teaching your child the name of a letter, but only teaching its sound. And there are countless videos and apps on teaching reading.

Let's look a little closer at what I found.

First, the videos and apps. Please, let's be real. Is your child really going to 'teach' him or herself to read?

Learning to read can be fun but wouldn't you say that learning to read is not exclusively a computer game?

Your child can read in one week – Think about that. If it were true, don't you think every school and tutoring center would be teaching that strategy? What *can* you do in one week? You can begin to build your sight and subject word vocabulary or learn a vowel sound, *but be able to read? No.*

Your one-year-old can read – Wouldn't you agree that at one year, your child is learning how to walk, talk and discover the fascinating world around him/her? Wouldn't you agree that exposure to colors and subject words and reading to your child is definitely on the menu? But learning to read? *....not yet.*

Reading is a natural process that does not need to be 'taught' – Really? Reading is the teaching and mastery of a compliment of skills. Isn't it true that like all skills, reading skills need to be taught?

All these well-meaning avenues do include several of the skills needed for your child to learn to read, but to my mind, just enough to be dangerous to the parent wanting the best for their child. Let's be candid, Reading is One of The MOST IMPORTANT skills you will ever have. Do you really think that it can be mastered virtually overnight?

Reading terms – Reading, like all subjects, has terminology. Sight words, CVC, word families, whole language. They are all important, they are all interconnected, but they are not 'magic' words. Not all words are sight words or have three letters and not all words belong to 'families.' Do you think you can pick one and say – 'My child can do that, so now my child can read?'

The overuse and implied simplification of these concepts distorts the importance of 'learning to read'. They are all avenues of ways to start to learn to read. But they are not 'stand-alone' nor exclusive as so much of the content out there is leading parents to believe. Each one of those is a 'piece'. Can we agree that you need more than just one piece to read?

Let me be honest, which is something I did not see anyone be with parents: Learning to read can include fun activities but learning to read is multi-faceted and intricate.

Teaching your child to read is not easy. Learning to read takes time. There are no shortcuts.

Teaching your child to read takes planning, preparation, and great materials. Most of all it takes perseverance, commitment, and time regardless of which method you choose.

Learning to read opens doors in a child's mind and allows them access to many fascinating worlds. Wouldn't you say that reading is necessary for just about everything that we do in life?

That opens the door to this next question:

What exactly is reading?

The Definition of Reading

It seems, that there are as many definitions of reading as there are experts, but for me, this is the only definition:

Reading is the ability to READ the WORDS AND COMPREHEND what the words say.

Why is this my only definition? Ask yourself these two questions:

1. If you are reading, but can't read all the words... *Can you read?*

2. If you can read the words, but don't understand what you are reading.... *Are you reading?*

Can you see why you need both parts? How one part cannot work without the other and how they are inter-connected?

Within this definition there are two ability levels. Each includes word mechanics and selection comprehension. The difference comes in how you are reading and how it is assessed.

Level 1: The ability to read *orally*, words that are familiar and unfamiliar in sentence or paragraph form AND the ability to 'tell back' what was read.

Level 2: The ability to read both familiar and unfamiliar words *silently* and then to recall or 'tell back' what was read, in writing.

Once a child masters the skills above and melds them together with accuracy......THEN and only then, is your child reading.

I have been asked...what is an 'unfamiliar word'? An unfamiliar word is a word that is not known immediately by sight or memorized. Therefore, you must 'decode' it to figure it out. Why is that important to be able to do? Think about this...can you memorize every word in the English language?

Ready to get started?

When Should you Start to Teach your Child to Read?

One of the most frequently asked questions by parents is at what age can I start to teach my child to read? *The answer: as early as possible.*

But what defines 'as early as possible?' Understanding the ramifications of this question can make all the difference to developing and nurturing a successful reader.

The biggest challenge for parents is to remember what 'reading' really is. There are those that say, "my two-year-old is reading'…. *but are they?*

For the most part, these young learners are repeating back the words and phrases that they have memorized. They are holding a book, usually one that has been read to them many times, turning the pages, and 'reading' the words, according to their parents.

As wonderful as that is, and it is a great accomplishment. Is that reading? No. They are reciting, they are not reading.

At what age can you start to teach your child to read?

To start the process of *Learning to Read*, your child needs the ability to do three things. **First,** they need to know all the letters of the alphabet, both lower case and capital, in isolation. Isolation being, they recognize the letters in a 'stand-alone' situation, not as part of saying the ABC song.

Second, they need to know the sound that each of those letters make. And **lastly**, they need the ability to sit for between twenty to thirty minutes to learn, to listen and to complete an assignment.

Once your child can do these three things…. Then, your child is ready to learn to read.

At what age does this happen? All children are different, but on average between three and a half and five years of age.

Does that mean that we wait to start to 'teach our children to read' until they are ready? Absolutely not! What we are doing, as early as possible, is to **PREPARE our children to read.** Build the foundation. So, when the time comes that they are READY to read, they will have the best experience possible.

How Should you Prepare your Child to Read?

Let's explore how we can prepare our children to become wonderful readers.

The First Step – *preparation*

I like to compare the teaching of reading to building a house. Preparation is synonymous with foundation. With preparation, you are pouring a strong foundation to build reading skills on.

This foundation, when done effectively *prior to kindergarten*, is invaluable to the child and will set them up for reading success!

Preparing your child to read starts as soon as they are born. Yes, even your newborn can start preparing for the eventuality of learning to read. Your baby is listening to your voice as you speak and sing to them. They absorb the tone, the rhythm, the starts and stops of what you are saying and singing. *(don't worry about your voice...sing away! Your child will love it!)* Comprehension and fluency are just that. Starts, stops, pauses and tone quality.

Read to your child. Develop and instill a love for reading and stories. Open their minds to the adventures they can have every time a book is opened. Board books, sensory books, and books that rhyme are the perfect start for your little ones. Teach them to turn the pages so they can be involved with you as you read.

As your child grows, they can start to develop 'sight words'. As you read, you can ask them to start 'identifying' words. They will think it's fun. You will know that you are starting their reading education. *Can you see the groundwork forming?*

Teach them nursery rhymes. I can't stress how important nursery rhymes are. Mary had a little lamb, Twinkle twinkle little star, Row, row, row your boat, etc.

The repetitive blending of words and sounds. Hearing the rhyme and rhythm of the words is the beginning of developing your child's ability to rhyme.

The ability to rhyme is one of the most important reading skills. For if your child can rhyme, your child can blend letters. If you can blend letters, you can start to read words.

The ability to rhyme is so important that I teach an entire unit of it – *Rhyme to Read*

A Rhyme to Read Workbook is available on our website: TheReadingSuperstars.com

The Next Step

Before a child can learn to read, they must **recognize all the letters of the alphabet**.

We all teach the ABC song to our children. It is a wonderful song, and it has its purpose. But your children must be able to recognize each letter, both capital and lower case *in isolation.*

This learning can be both formal and informal. For formal, flash cards. Informal, there are letters everywhere you go. A stop sign, a store sign, the labels on a can at the grocery store, the license plates on your car. Learning to recognize letters is fun. The more fun you can make it, the more excited your child will be. The more excited the child...the faster the learning.

Once they can recognize the letters, they need to learn the **sounds that each of the letters make**. There are several options available - Workbooks, internet classes, computer programs. My favorite is my own *StoryTime Letters*. A complete developmental program that teaches letter sounds through both visual and auditory activities and the fun of stories.

Storytime Letters is available on our website. TheReadingSuperstars.com

The last step is to start building their **sight and subject words**. Sight words are words that your children 'need to know by sight' ex: the, was, are. Most sight words cannot be figured out and must be memorized. Flash cards work best. Subject words can be easily pictured ex: boy, girl, house. You can start learning to read sight and subject words once your child recognizes their letters.

Two ideas to try…. start with the names of colors. Red, blue, green, yellow etc. Make two sets of flash cards. One that has a picture of the color on the front and the word underneath the color. Second, a picture of the color on the front, the word on the back. These cards are great for both recognizing colors and reading color names.

When my children were learning to read, I put pictures of subject words (cat, dog, bird, etc) on the wall. I made matching word cards. Matching the word to the picture became a nightly game.

Can you see how you can make learning fun? Incorporate 'word' learning into your daily routine. Your child will be 'reading words' in no time.

Ready to move on to the next stage?

The Reading Process

There are many different views and programs on learning to read. All of them are viable, have merit and have been designed by experts.

There are facets that will overlap and intersect in each of them, for basics are basics and you must have the basics to read.

The differences come in which road they follow and how they follow it.

There are four major reading model designs. Within each of these there are different programs or variations, but the underlying approach of the variation would reflect the reading model they are based on.

The four models are:

1. Whole Language
2. CVC
3. Spelling Patterns to Read
4. Phonics

Let's look briefly at each one.

Please remember that this book reflects my view and my opinion based on many years of teaching many children.

Whole Language

Whole language is the teaching of 'whole words'. That is a fancy way of saying that you need to memorize every word.

The story lessons are fun. The stories are cute. They are presented in Big Books with smaller books for follow-up and there is much repetition in words. This repetition in words along with great pictures makes 'memorizing the story' easy, so when the kids pick up the corresponding small books on their own, they think they are reading.

This method, for me, is an offshoot of Sight Words. You introduce the story words, and the children memorize them. Sight words are very important, but you cannot memorize every word in the English language. So, what do you do when you get stuck and don't know a word? Kids tend to 'skip over' the words they do not know, and as a result will not understand what they have read, because they did not read the entire passage.

So, for me, the 'whole language' approach will not work. *It does not give you the skills you need to 'figure out' words that are unfamiliar.*

CVC

An important, and very overused term. What it means is Consonant, Vowel, Consonant. Example: cat, dog, big, top etc. Yes, we start learning in small steps, and the CVC format is the choice for the start of most reading programs, but what happens when you get to a word like: flip or bend? What happens when you have multiple syllables? Not every word will fit the pattern, and you will see exceptions very quickly. CVC is a great starting point and a very important piece of the pie. But kids need more than this to become successful readers. Can we say that *One skill or piece is not enough?*

Spell to Read

Spelling is very important, even in the age of our amazing technology. But to focus on 'spelling patterns' ex: spelling CVC pattern or spelling long vowel and long vowel combination patterns or spelling blend and digraph patterns are not the 'teaching of skill sets' that will allow our children to read words, familiar or unfamiliar.

Again, spelling is a piece of the pie. But don't you need more than just one piece?

PHONICS

Phonics is the teaching of skills. It is the 'building of skill sets', that will enable your child to 'decode' or 'attack' a word that is unfamiliar and figure it out.

Phonics starts with the teaching of the sounds of consonants. It then teaches in '**building block formation'** vowels, blends, and digraphs. Phonics will teach your child to read the simple, CVC like *cat,* to the complex of breaking words into syllables, so they can 'decode and read' words like *wonderful, fantastic, mountain and monster.*

There is a key phrase above: *Building block formation.* I can rename this as the 'building of skill sets.' Each skill set is a piece. All the pieces will give your child the entire pie! *And isn't that nice!*

Back to my analogy for the teaching of reading is to compare it to the building of a house. First, you need to pour the foundation. Then you can build the first floor, then the second etc. If each floor is strong and secure, you can build upon it. The result – a strong house. *Phonics gives your child all the building blocks for a strong house.*

My choice of reading program – PHONICS BASED.

The Reading Superstars Program

There are several phonics-based programs available, including mine. In fact, when I started teaching first grade, I was using a phonics-based program. But I found that I needed more. My students were not 'getting it' through the traditional phonetic process.

I looked at other phonics programs, but I could not find the answers I needed. One evening, I was telling my dad about my concerns. My dad said: 'Look carefully and analyze what is right in front of you. The answer will be there if you look.' *Smart man, my dad.* So, I looked.

I started to analyze from the beginning.

1. Know and recognize each of the letters, both lower case and capital in isolation.
2. Know the sound that each letter makes.
3. Sound out the word, starting with the sound of the first letter.

And there it was. The little thing that changed the lives of so many of my kids. And by making that change, the kids who could not read, began to read. Those who were progressing nicely, progressed faster.

What did I do? It was so simple, thank you dad!
Let's look at the word 'cat'

Traditional process: sound out one letter at a time starting with the first. I will attempt to sound this out in writing. The kids would go: CU A T the sounds of the letters c, a and t. They did not end up saying the word cat. When you look further, what you really need to do, is NOT sound out the individual letter sounds but BLEND the sounds, starting with the first TWO letters as one. THEN, you will say **ca** t – cat

Great! But what happens when the kids can't blend? No one teaches blending. It is expected. But when you are teaching you should not expect anything. You teach it.

How do you teach blending? The answer comes in its definition. What is blending? Blending is rhyming! *Can you see why I put such an emphasis on that skill?*

I went back to nursery rhymes. Why nursery rhymes? They rhyme and to learn to rhyme you must hear the rhyme. We went from nursery rhymes to nonsense words. From nonsense words to blending letter sounds. We were on the right track.

But it was not smooth sailing. It was all good in short vowels, but we hit a large barrier when we got to long vowels. Ex: pet was no problem, but Pete was. So now what do I do?

Again, *look and analyze.* And what I found became the basis of the entire Reading Superstars program. **And it works....**

EVERY TIME! With every vowel, with just about *every* decodable word and with just about *every* child. *What did I find?....*

Figuring out a word is DEPENDANT on the vowel.

I started to teach a 'decoding process'.

1. Start with the VOWEL,
2. Rhyme the first letter,
3. then add the last letter.

So simple, so perfect! The word cat – what is the vowel? A What sound does it make – a, rhyme with the first letter - ca, add the last letter – cat.

Let's go back to our pet and Pete.
Pet – the vowel is e – is it short or long?
Answer – short. Decode the word: e, pe, pet

Pete – what is the vowel? e – is short or long? Answer - Long, because there is a magic e at the end. Decode the word – e, Pe, Pete.

Once the VOWEL was identified, the kids just followed the process. They ALWAYS ended up saying the correct word! *Can you see how the reading superstars decoding process was helping the kids succeed?*

Works EVERY TIME! Short vowels, long vowels, vowel combinations. Further along in the year, breaking larger words into syllables is dependent on the vowel. I could put any word on the board –wonderful, mountain, exclaim, suppose *(and not just first grade words...**ANY words**)*. The kids could figure them all out. I did not have to teach them. What I did do is *give them the phonetic and blending skills to 'figure out' any word they saw.* And the exceptions? – they started with the rule, and if it didn't sound right, they knew to change the vowel sound from short to long or vice versa.

Can you see how the 'decoding process' increases their reading abilities?

The Reading Superstar Program will give you:
* **Reading Building Blocks for Success**
* **Happy Kids**
* **Successful Readers!**

And isn't that the result we want?

A question that I have been asked, is will the kids always have to start with the vowel to read and figure out words?

Answer: As your children become confident readers, the procedures for decoding will start to become 'instinctive' and they will automatically process from the beginning. There will be times that they will go back to isolating the vowel with larger words that need to be broken into syllables, but even then, once the skill has become 'ingrained', most will automatically see and use it.

The Building Blocks for Success

The Reading Superstars Map

As I said when this book started, the most successful people in any business and coaches who help their clients make millions of dollars will tell you that there is a map you must follow to be successful. The same applies to the teaching of reading.

The Reading Superstars provides the map and the materials you will need. It is based on phonetic building blocks and the "building a house' analogy I introduced earlier.

A. Foundation

1. Learn to Rhyme
    Materials: Workbook: Rhyme to Read

2. Learn the names of letters, both capital and lowercase, in isolation.

3. Learn the sounds of the letters.
    Materials – Storytime Letter Program

4. Sight Words - *ongoing*
   Materials: Workbooks: Learn to Read Sight Words

   a. These are words that many refer to as High Frequency words. Most sight words are not 'decodable' and must be memorized.
   b. Sight words are instrumental for Reading Fluency
   c. The Reading Superstars Sight Word books include word introduction, writing, reading comprehension and assessment.

5. Subject Words- *ongoing*
   a. Build your vocabulary of easily recognized items.

B. <u>Build your house one floor at a time.</u>

Learn your skill Sets **IN ORDER.** Don't go on until the skill you are working on has been mastered.
Materials: Learn to Decode Workbooks. There is one complete workbook for each vowel letter.

1. First floor: learn to read and decode **short vowel words.**

2. Second floor: learn to read and decode **long vowel words.**

3. Add windows: learn to read **blends** and **digraphs.**

4. Third floor - learn to break words into **syllables** and read and recognize **compound words.**

And... learn and practice your sight and subject words for fluency EVERYDAY!

My class would start every day with lists of words on the board. The kids would read the words, circle words and their favorite – read to disappear - after they read the word or the list, they could erase it. They had fun. They even had contests to see who could read a list fastest! *Can you see how we were building sight and subject word fluency?*

Essentials for Reading Comprehension

Up until now, we have been talking about the Mechanics of Reading. – *The ability to read words.*

Comprehension is the ability to understand what you are reading and in my building a house analogy, *putting on the roof.*

Comprehension is NOT automatic. It may seem automatic to you if your child is reading the words, but it is not necessarily automatic to your child. Comprehension must be taught. Your child needs to learn how to *'think and read'*.

I had a boy in my class. During a conference, his mom said, 'he can read everything, so why isn't getting 100% on his reading tests?' Yes, he could read every word, but I found that he was not processing what he was reading. *He needed to be taught how to 'think and read' at the same time.* Can you see why that skill is necessary?

The next day, I started incorporating 'think and read' worksheets with my class.

These fun worksheets increased the comprehension skills of ALL my students. It was like a light bulb that was just turned on.

The Guide to Teaching Reading Comprehension

First Step: The Reading Superstars – *Think and Read workbook*. This book should be started after the completion of *Learn to Read Sight Words Book 1* and with the finishing of at least Decoding Short a. Use the book in order, as the skill level of the worksheets increases as you go. *You will be building reading confidence and training your child's mind to 'think and read.'*

First Step Readers

Kids love to hold and read books. They also need to see that all the work they are doing is 'paying off'.

First Step Readers are short storybooks that are PHONICS BASED and complement *The Reading Superstars* program. Once you finish learning a vowel sound, read that vowel *First Step Reader*. Every word in the book is either a sight word, or a decodable that they are working on or have been introduced to. This is specifically done to build fluency and confidence. Each story has a skill and comprehension activity packet for assessment. *Can you see the building block strategy? Word skills and comprehension intertwined.*

Reading Comprehension Workbooks

There are several reading comprehension workbooks available. Most offer on one page both reading selection and a couple of comprehension questions. To my way of thinking, those suffice as a quick assessment or homework assignment, but they do not teach reading comprehension.

Reading comprehension is a skill, and skills need to be taught. And wouldn't you agree that the more competent the child is with the skill, the stronger the reader they will be?

The Reading Superstars books were designed to TEACH reading comprehension. Each selection is on its own page. The selections are vocabulary controlled for ease of reading. They promote fluency and confidence.

Each reading selection includes:

- Step One: Brainstorming to focus your mind on what you are about to read.
- Step Two: Vocabulary for ease of reading
- Step Three: A Fun reading selection
- Step Four: comprehension activity.

Use the book in order as the skill level increases as you go. Gentle increases = stronger readers!

Just for Fun Reading Comprehension Workbook

Sometimes, reading comprehension should be just for fun. These are one page fun reading selections followed by a separate page of comprehension questions. These stories make great 'extra credit', homework or assessment or Just for FUN!

Ability Graded Readers – *Superstar Readers*

Kids love books. They especially love picture books. But picture books were not written for kids to read. Picture books are written for parents to read to kids. There are beginner readers available in a step series. They are good. But so many kids want the books to have a story that they can relate to with the beauty of a picture book.

Superstar Readers fill in the gap between the step reader and the chapter books. They are kid focused stories in a close to picture book format. These books are easy to read, and several teach a lesson ex: be a good friend, believe in yourself, do your best and some are just fun. Enjoy having your child read them to you! *Won't that be fun?*

All referenced material is available on our website. TheReadingSuperstars.com

Enjoy Your Child

I hope that I have been able to give you both perspective and insight into the meaning and process of learning to read.

Preparing your children to read is fun! Teaching your child to read is exciting! Choose the path and follow the map, one step at a time.

Learning to read is not quick, it is not easy. But the result is priceless.

Learning to read is a process that your child needs to be ready for. It cannot be 'rushed'. Just like your child will walk when they are ready, they will learn to read when they are ready. A note of caution: children learn at different paces. Know when to stop a lesson and give them, and yourself, a break. The skill will come. Be patient with them and yourself.

Most importantly, enjoy reading with your child. Find books on topics they will enjoy. Show them how much fun reading can be. If it is fun for them, they will develop a love for reading.

Place their feet firmly on the road to becoming successful readers.

And isn't that our fondest wish for them?

Teddy Bear Readers

From the very beginning, reading should be a wonderful experience. When your child is a newborn, through infant, you might be reading the books you fell in love with when you were a child. This is followed and complimented by wonderful board books, that they can handle – turn the pages, 'feel' those that are sensory, etc.

Then, comes the beginning of reading skills – *Teddy Bear readers* were designed for this stage. They are hardcover books that will help develop beginning skills – rhyme, ABC, counting etc. They are fun, colorful books and many of them are interactive! They come with a cuddly stuffed animal that you can make with your child. *(Stuffed animals are approved for ages 3 +).* They make a wonderful reading experience for you and your child...enjoy them all.

Teddy Bear Readers are available on our website. TheReadingSuperstars.com

Thank you for reading; *Want Your Child to Read?*

It is my fondest wish to help as many children as possible learn to become great readers and enjoy reading *and* to offer parents an easy, step-by-step map to follow.

My best wishes for your success.

Laurie

My Gift to You

The Reading Superstars series provides a great map with awesome workbooks and readers to help teach your child to read.

To introduce you to the series, go to our website, www.TheReadingSuperstars.com and enter the word READING in the discount code box.

This will save your $ 5.00 on orders of $ 20.00 or more.

www.ingramcontent.com/pod-product-compliance
Lightning Source LLC
Chambersburg PA
CBHW020347130626
46549CB00003B/1335